From Caterpillar to
BUTTERFLY

by **Deborah Heiligman** illustrated by **Bari Weissman**

HarperCollins*Publishers*

For Aaron and all the children
of Wrightstown Friends Nursery School.

With special thanks to their teachers,
Marty Severn, Tina Hayden, and Karen Pearson,
who grow beautiful butterflies and then let them go.
Many thanks also to Louis Sorkin for his expert advice.

The *Let's-Read-and-Find-Out Science* book series was originated by Dr. Franklyn M. Branley, Astronomer Emeritus and former Chairman of the American Museum–Hayden Planetarium, and was formerly co-edited by him and Dr. Roma Gans, Professor Emeritus of Childhood Education, Teachers College, Columbia University. Text and illustrations for each of the books in the series are checked for accuracy by an expert in the relevant field. For more information about Let's-Read-and-Find-Out Science books, write to HarperCollins Children's Books, 10 East 53rd Street, New York, NY 10022.

Library of Congress Cataloging-in-Publication Data
Heiligman, Deborah.
   From caterpillar to butterfly / by Deborah Heiligman ; illustrated by Bari Weissman.
       p.   cm. — (Let's-read-and-find-out science. Stage 1)
       ISBN 0-06-024264-7. — ISBN 0-06-024268-X (lib. bdg.)
       ISBN 0-06-445129-1 (pbk.)
       1. Butterflies—Metamorphosis—Juvenile literature.
   2. Caterpillars—Juvenile literature.   [1. Butterflies—Metamorphosis.
   2. Metamorphosis.   3. Caterpillars.]   I. Weissman, Bari, ill.
   II. Title.   III. Series.
   QL544.2.H44   1996   93-39055
   595.78'904334—dc20   CIP
                                                               AC

Typography by Elynn Cohen

From Caterpillar to
BUTTERFLY

4

Today a caterpillar came to school in a jar. It is eating green leaves. It is climbing and wiggling. This tiny caterpillar is going to change. It will change into a beautiful butterfly.

Caterpillars usually turn into butterflies outdoors. They live in gardens and meadows and yards. But we will watch our caterpillar change into a butterfly right here in our classroom. This change is called metamorphosis.

A butterfly is an insect.

Our caterpillar started out as a tiny egg. The mother butterfly laid the egg on a leaf.

The egg is tiny. It is the size of a pinhead.

When the caterpillar hatched out of the egg,
it was hungry. It ate its way out of its own eggshell!
Then it started to eat green plants right away.

The mother butterfly lays her eggs on plants that the caterpillar will eat. These are called host plants.

The
caterpillar
is also called
the larva.

A caterpillar's job is to eat and eat and eat,
so it will grow and grow and grow.

Each day when we come into school, we look
at our caterpillar. Each day it is bigger.

12

The caterpillar eats and grows for 12 to 14 days.

13

Our skin grows with us. But a caterpillar's skin does not grow. When the caterpillar gets too big for its skin, the skin splits down the back.

The caterpillar crawls right out of its own skin. It has new skin underneath. This is called molting. Our caterpillar will molt four or five times.

After many days our caterpillar is
finished growing. It is much bigger than when it
first came to school. It is almost as big as my little finger now.

Our caterpillar is making a special house. First it makes a button of silk.

Button of silk

It uses this button to hang upside down from a twig. Then it molts for the last time. Instead of a new skin, this time there is a hard shell. This shell is called a chrysalis. Our caterpillar will stay inside the chrysalis for a long time.

Chrysalis

The chrysalis is also called the pupa.

Every day the chrysalis looks the same. We can't see anything happening. But inside the chrysalis our caterpillar is changing.

The caterpillar stays in the chrysalis about one week.

Will our caterpillar ever turn into a butterfly? Will it ever come out of its chrysalis? We can hardly wait. But we do. We wait and wait and wait.

Then, one day, during snack time, somebody shouts, "Look!" And we all rush over to see.

The chrysalis
is cracking.

We see a head,
a body,
and then . . . wings!

It's a butterfly!

The tiny caterpillar who came to school
in a jar turned into a Painted Lady butterfly!
And we saw it happen.

Our butterfly is damp and crumpled. It
hangs on to the chrysalis while its wings
flap, flap, flap. Blood pumps into its wings.
The wings straighten out and dry. Soon our
butterfly will be ready to fly.

In two hours the wings are dry and the butterfly is ready to fly.

Our butterfly cannot stay in the jar. It needs to be outside with flowers and grass and trees and other butterflies.

It is a warm spring day. I put my finger into the jar. The butterfly sits on my finger. I pull it out and our butterfly goes free. We feel a little sad and a little happy.

We watch our butterfly land on a flower. It will sip the flower's nectar through a long, coiled tube called a proboscis. Maybe it is a female butterfly. Maybe someday she will lay an egg on a leaf.

I know just what will happen then. That egg will hatch into a caterpillar. And that caterpillar will turn into a beautiful butterfly.

Painted Lady butterflies sip nectar from certain flowers. They like thistle, burdock, zinnia, butterfly bush, and mint.

How many different kinds of butterflies can you find around your neighborhood? Here are some common ones to look for.

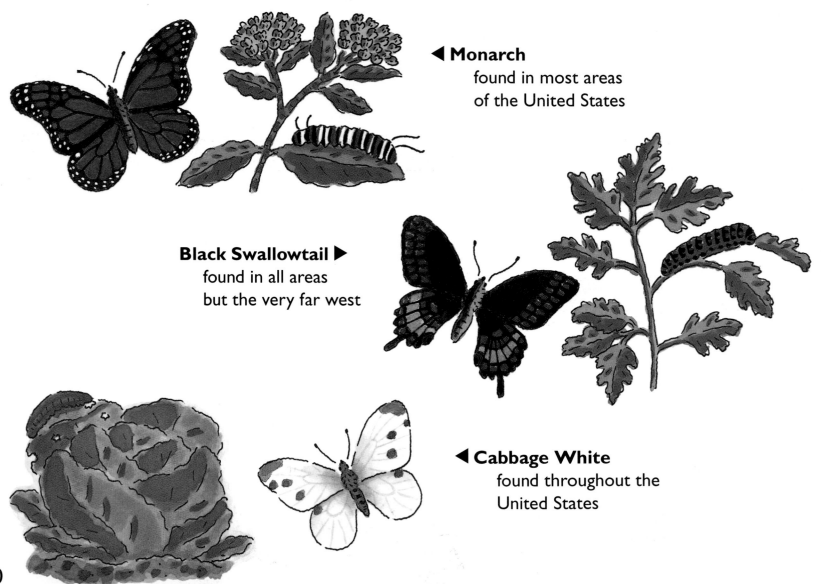

◀ **Monarch**
found in most areas
of the United States

Black Swallowtail ▶
found in all areas
but the very far west

◀ **Cabbage White**
found throughout the
United States

Dogface Butterfly ▶
found throughout the south;
migrates through the midwest to
the northeast and Canada

◀ Common Blue
found in the western
part of the United States

Buckeye ▶
found in most areas of the
United States except for the
Pacific Northwest

31

Here are some places to see butterflies:

The Butterfly Place
120 Tyngsboro Road
Westford, MA 01886
(508) 392-0955

Day Butterfly Center
Callaway Gardens
Pine Mountain, GA 31822
(706) 663-5102

Butterfly World
Tradewinds Park South
3600 West Sample Road
Coconut Creek, FL 33073
(305) 977- 4434

Marine World Africa—U.S.A.
Butterfly Exhibit
Marine World Parkway
Vallejo, CA 94589
(707) 644-4000